DATE DUE

MAR 2 5 ANSO	ully Acuña 301	

Animals All Around

Do Cows Eat Cake?

A Book About What Animals Eat

Written by Michael Dahl
Illustrated by Sandra D'Antonio

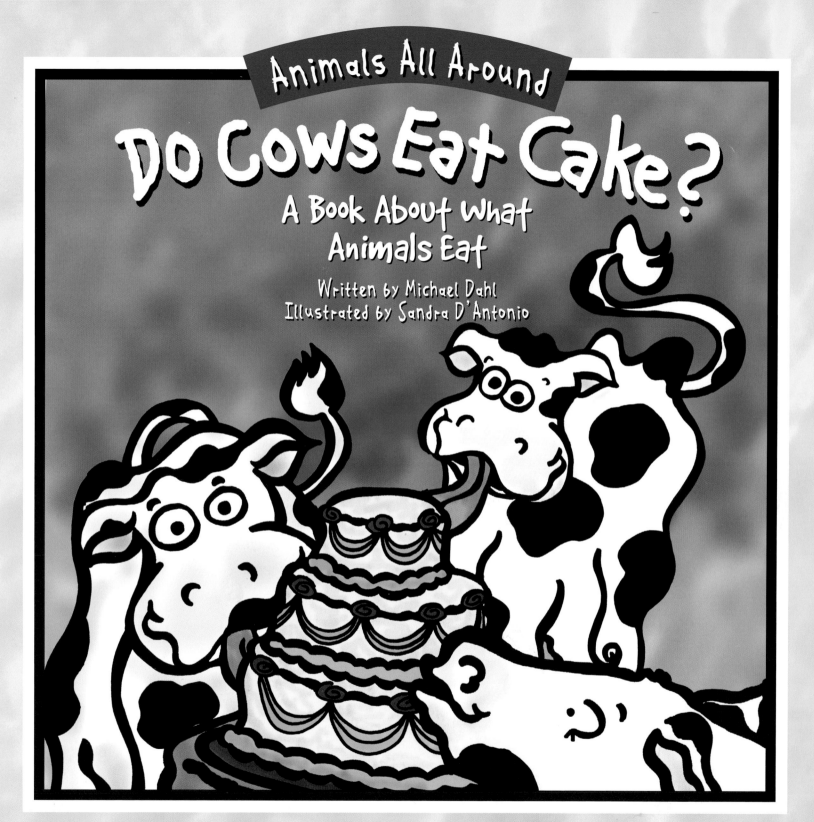

Content Consultant: Kathleen E. Hunt, Ph.D.
Research Scientist and Lecturer, Zoology Department
University of Washington, Seattle, Washington

Reading Consultant: Susan Kesselring, M.A., Literacy Educator
Rosemount-Apple Valley-Eagan (Minnesota) School District

PICTURE WINDOW BOOKS
MINNEAPOLIS, MINNESOTA

Animals All Around series editor: Peggy Henrikson
Page production: The Design Lab
The illustrations in this book were rendered in marker.

Picture Window Books
5115 Excelsior Boulevard
Suite 232
Minneapolis, MN 55416
1-877-845-8392
www.picturewindowbooks.com

Printed in the United States of America.
1 2 3 4 5 6 08 07 06 05 04 03

Library of Congress Cataloging-in-Publication Data
Dahl, Michael.
Do cows eat cake? / written by Michael Dahl ; illustrated by
Sandra D'Antonio.
p. cm. — (Animals all around)
Summary: Introduces a number of different animals and the
foods they eat.
ISBN 1-4048-0101-4 (lib. bdg.)
1. Animals—Food—Juvenile literature. [1. Animals—Food.]
I. D'Antonio, Sandra, 1956— ill. II. Title.
QL756.5 .D34 2003
591.53—dc21
2002155016

No! Cows eat grass.

Cows graze on grass in green meadows. They also eat clover, peas, corn, and hay. Cows chew and swallow their food, then they bring it up later to chew it some more. This partly chewed food is called cud.

Do sharks eat cake?

No! Sharks eat fish.

Sharks are giant ocean fish that eat smaller fish. Sharks have 5 to 15 rows of sharp teeth that can bite through bone.

Do giraffes eat cake?

No! Giraffes eat leaves.

Giraffes lift their long necks into the branches of tall trees. They nibble leaves that other animals cannot reach. A giraffe's tongue can slip between thorny branches and twist around a tasty bud.

Do monkeys eat cake?

No! Monkeys eat mangoes.

Monkeys scramble up fruit trees to pluck sweet mangoes and tear them open. Monkeys also eat leaves and flowers. A frog, lizard, bat, or bug might become a monkey's meal.

Do rabbits eat cake?

No! Rabbits eat carrots.

Rabbits and bunnies eat carrots as a special treat. Wild rabbits eat mostly green, leafy plants. In winter, when green leaves are scarce, hungry rabbits will eat twigs and tree bark.

Do whales eat cake?

No! Whales eat squid.

Orca whales are good hunters. Besides squiggly squid, orcas eat fish, turtles, and seals. They even eat sea birds when they can catch them.

Do anteaters eat cake?

No! Anteaters eat ants.

Anteaters rip open anthills with their sharp claws. Their long, sticky tongues dart out and snatch up the scurrying ants. An anteater's wiggling tongue can worm its way deep into ant tunnels to find even more food.

Do pandas eat cake?

No! Pandas eat bamboo.

Pandas have special front paws with bony thumbs. These thumbs are good for gripping stiff bamboo stems. Powerful panda jaws and teeth crunch through the stems and chew the tough roots.

Do raccoons eat cake?

No! Raccoons eat berries.

Raccoons ramble through berry bushes, picking berries with their hand-like paws. They also eat seeds, nuts, eggs, and fruit. Raccoons have a great sense of touch. They can find fish, frogs, and crayfish by reaching into rivers and streams.

Do kids eat cake?

Yes! Kids eat cake.
Kids eat veggies and bread.
Kids eat berries and meat.
Kids eat lots of the same food that animals eat.
Kids eat food that is broiled or boiled or baked,
and on special days, kids eat plenty of cake!

What Animals Eat

Animals eat soft things.

tangy berries	raccoons
squishy mangoes	monkeys
green grass	cows

Animals eat hard things.

chewy bamboo	pandas
crunchy carrots	rabbits

Animals eat things that wiggle and move.

slippery fish	sharks
squiggly squid	whales
creepy-crawly ants	anteaters

Animals eat food that grows up high.

tasty leaves on tall, tall trees	giraffes

Words to Know

anthill—a little hill of dirt made by ants when they dig their tunnels in the earth

bamboo—tall, stick-like plants with hard, hollow stems

bud—tightly closed flower or leaf that has not yet opened

clover—small, leafy plants that grow low to the ground

cud—partly chewed and swallowed food that a cow brings up again to chew some more

scarce—hard to find. Leaves on trees are scarce during the winter.

squid—a long, narrow sea animal that has ten, waving arms

Index

To Learn More

At the Library

Arno, Iris Hiskey. *I Like a Snack on an Iceberg*. New York: HarperFestival, 1999.

Arnold, Caroline. *Mealtime for Zoo Animals*. Minneapolis: Carolrhoda Books, 1999.

Facklam, Margery. *Bugs for Lunch*. Watertown, Mass.: Charlesbridge, 1999.

London, Jonathan. *Crunch Munch*. San Diego: Silver Whistle/Harcourt, 2001.

On the Web

Minnesota Zoo
http://www.mnzoo.com/index.asp
Explore the Minnesota Zoo online, including a Family Farm. See pictures of the animals and visit the Kids' Corner with animal puzzles, games, and coloring sheets.

Zoological Society of San Diego: e-zoo
http://www.sandiegozoo.org/virtualzoo/homepage.html
Visit this virtual zoo with a Kid Territory. The section for kids includes animal profiles, games, zoo crafts, and even animal-theme recipes, such as Warthog Waffles.

Want to learn more about what animals eat?
Visit FACT HOUND at http://www.facthound.com.